WHAT MID-LIFE CRISIS?
ENTERING A NEW STAGE OF LIFE

What Mid-Life Crisis?
Entering a New Stage of Life

Celia Dawson

What Mid-Life Crisis?: Entering a New Stage of Life

© Celia Dawson

ISBN 978-1-906316-08-2

All rights reserved. No part of this publication may be reproduced, stored in a retrieval system, or transmitted in any form or by any means, electronic, mechanical, photocopying, recording or otherwise, without the prior permission of the copyright holder.

A copy of this publication has been registered with the British Library.

Published by Word4Word in 2008
8 King Charles Court, Evesham, Worcestershire
www.w4wdp.com

Printed in the UK by Cromwell Press, Trowbridge

Contents

Foreword	v
Stepping Into a New Way of Being	1
Men at Mid-Life	7
Women at Mid-Life	21
Marriage and Partnerships	31
Depression and Breakdown	53
Family Roles	59
Where Do We Go From Here?	67
Bibliography	81
About the Author	83

Foreword

In writing this book I have, by its very nature, been obliged to make generalisations. It would be impossible to encompass the range of experiences and life conditions of everyone in this age group.

I hope, therefore, I will be forgiven if I seem callous or neglectful of people who are in especially difficult circumstances. This book is meant for the majority.

The case studies I have used are fictional.

Stepping Into a New Way of Being

The mid-life crisis is a new phenomenon. In 1900 the average life span was only fifty years. Many children died in infancy, mothers died in childbirth and we did not have modern medicine. Very few people lived to old age. Modern life is so different. Nowadays we can expect to live at least until we are 75 and increasing numbers of people live into their eighties and nineties. And people in their mid-life years aren't old as they used to be. They are still energetic and active, and many are still attractive. They wear modern clothes and still live very much in the modern world. They are not fading away as older people used to do.

Going through life we pass through different stages. Everybody knows about the difficulties of adolescence. Adolescence isn't considered to be a crisis; it is accepted as a normal stage of growing up. It is a time when young people examine the traditions, beliefs and values of their parents and then decide what they should keep and what they need to change so that they can become their own individual person. Our peers are very important to us in our teens. We meet new people from different backgrounds and we learn that there are different ways to be and to live. Sometimes young people throw out the whole lot – all of their parents' morals and values. It is a time of experimentation. They sometimes get into trouble but most young people settle down by the time they reach their early twenties. They get through the rough patch somehow and learn from their experiences.

The next stage for most people is their twenties and thirties. During these years their priorities are to establish themselves with a career and a home and to bring up children. This is a time, especially for men, when it is important to get as high as possible up the ladder and make as much money as possible. For many women with children their time is taken up with juggling the competing demands of work and children.

The big question is, 'What happens next?' We have brought up our children, many of us have established careers; people at mid-life are usually better off financially than they have ever been. But there is the other half of our life still to live. What do we do with it? Mid-life, like adolescence, is a time for re-evaluation. We suddenly become aware of death. People around us begin to die, our parents become frail. We start to think about what we have done with our life so far. What will we have to show for it when we die? What is the point of it all anyway?

So What Happens at Mid-Life?

Capitalism is fine for young people. It has led to prosperity and comfort in the Western world and is beginning to help the poorer nations to become richer. It is because of this system bringing better nutrition and health that we now have such a huge number of middle-aged people who are likely to survive into their eighties and nineties. But people are finding that the beliefs and values of capitalism are not enough. The crisis comes when we find that we are at odds with this culture. We are trying to carry on as we did before but it just isn't working. As Jung puts it, 'Thoroughly unprepared we take the step into the afternoon of life; worse still, we take this step with the false presupposition that our truths and ideals will serve us as hitherto' (Jung, 2001). It no longer seems sufficient to be part of the machine, to spend our lives working hard to sell things to one another. There is an uneasy feeling that there must be more to life. And as we start to get older we wonder what will happen when our children are grown up, what will be the point of working so hard when there is no family to support. Jane Polden's parody of Descartes, 'I work, I shop, I keep the economy going, therefore I am' (Polden, 2002), sums up the dilemma.

By mid-life people will either have reached the pinnacle of success or will know that they never will succeed at what they wanted to do. Making money no longer seems to be so important. We can't take our new Jaguar or six-bedroomed house with us when we pass through the pearly gates. We have spent our lives trying to do what was expected of us. But in a culture that is serving the great god Capitalism, if we question the status quo we are going against all the principles we have previously held dear, going against the grain of accepted wisdom. This is what frightens us.

We are suddenly aware that life is short and there are things we have always wanted to do that we haven't got around to yet. If we don't get on with it, it will be too late. The talents and abilities that we needed to function in a capitalist society have held sway for years but the other parts of us, our creativity, our connection to the Earth, our intuitive senses, have not had a chance to develop. Eventually these parts start to assert themselves, or try to. If we can't give them room to grow we will become stuck. We may break down, or depression will take hold, or bitterness, or we will become one of those tiresome old people who talk constantly about the past and find it difficult to cope with the present, let alone the future. We will grow old quickly and, without anything to nourish our spirit, we will die a premature death.

People at mid-life are finding that there are no patterns for their future. Since ancient Greek times man has followed the path of reason. Now we begin to realise that 'Our current modes of rationality are not moving society forward into a better world ... the whole structure of reason, handed down to us from ancient times, is no longer adequate. It begins to be seen for what it really is – emotionally hollow, aesthetically meaningless and spiritually empty' (Pirsig, 1974). Role models are few and far between. Religion is losing its power, churches are empty, but there seems to be nothing to fill the gap. Up until now there has always been a well-worn path trodden by others. Our goals have been clear. But now the path has petered out. There is a trackless wilderness out there. What direction should we take?

It may be scary but it is a huge opportunity. We are free to do anything we like. We have to establish a new culture, we have to be our own role models. We can

Stepping Into a New Way of Being

change the world if we want to. We have to find out what more there is to life, to tread new paths. We are the pioneers who have the difficult job of opening up the trackless wilderness. Maybe this time we can do it without ruining it.

Men at Mid-Life

Graham is 45. He runs a small department in a large building society where he has worked for the last twenty years, gradually rising up through the organisation. He has a four-bedroomed detached house in a pleasant modern development not far from his work. He has a wife and two children. The children are 17 and 15. Graham works very hard and often has to go in to work at weekends to prepare reports and make sure that everything is ready for Monday morning. He often works late in the evenings too. He thinks it is worthwhile because he is on quite a good salary. His work takes up most of his energy, so when he is at home he spends his time watching the television. He can afford to take the family on expensive holidays and they have been on all-inclusive holidays to the Caribbean for the last few years, though his elder daughter has now declared that she will be going on holiday with her own friends next year. Graham's wife, Sue, stayed at home with the children until they started school and then got a part-time job in the office of a small local firm.

Graham finds his job very absorbing. It is always very busy and he sometimes wonders how he can keep up with all the work. He could do with an assistant but his requests have always been blocked by those higher up. Often he gets angry and frustrated by his colleagues who don't seem to realise how important it is that everything should be done according to the procedures he has set up. After all, it is for the good of the organisation they are working for. He sometimes brings these frustrations home and will grumble and snap at Sue and the children. They respond by keeping their distance from him and leaving him to fall asleep in front of the television.

Graham is beginning to put on weight, which doesn't bother him too much, but he is worried that his hair is going grey and getting thin on top. He is beginning to get a little uneasy about his age but, after all, he has a good salary and a comfortable home. Life isn't too bad. Pity he has to spend such a lot of time at work, though. But work does have its compensations. He has noticed some cheeky looks from one of the receptionists. It is always a pleasure to exchange a little banter with her when he signs in in the mornings. It makes his day seem worthwhile. There is nothing in it, of course, he is happily married. But, come to think of it, Sue is getting a bit faded-looking. And they only have sex about once a month now, she doesn't seem to be interested any more . . .

Until he reaches mid-life everything around our man has been geared to support his position in society and his rise through the ranks. The ethics and values of modern society have served him well. He has been encouraged all along to work hard and do well in his job. The traditional role of his partner has been to subjugate her wants in order to service this progress. She has looked after the children and the domestic chores, so there has been nothing to distract him from his duty to earn money to provide for his family. His mortgage is almost paid, he has furnished his house and has a new car. Often he will have taken his partner for granted and neglected to build relationships with his children because he has been so busy 'making it'. Now he has got as far as he is going. His relationship has gone stale, his children have reached adolescence and are beginning to break away from their parents. They aren't interested in him any more. His partner is putting her energies into projects of her own and is no longer willing to give him all the attention he is used to receiving.

Five years later we find Graham's family falling apart. Graham has left Sue to live with Michelle, the receptionist from his work. At the moment they are living in a small rented house while Graham's family finances are being sorted out. He has sold his family car and bought a sports model. He loves driving around in it with Michelle, showing off. He is having a great time with Michelle, a wonderful sex life. He is learning all sorts of things about sex that he never imagined existed. Sue was so boring in bed; no wonder they didn't have sex very often. He is confidently expecting to move back into his family home once Sue and the children have moved out. After all, it was his money that bought the house. Sue will have to get a full-time job and find her own place to live.

What Mid-Life Crisis?

A lot of men when they reach mid-life suddenly realise that time is beginning to run out. When their bodies begin to show signs of ageing they start to panic. They have done everything that society has expected of them. At this age they are usually quite well-off financially: they have made a home and brought up a family. But now they are beginning to fall foul of the accepted norms portrayed by the media. They are losing their looks. The media is constantly presenting us with images of youth and beauty: we are faced with beautiful men and women everywhere on billboards, film and TV, in newspapers. Sex is everywhere. It is a constant subject of news, gossip and entertainment. We feel we have to aspire to be everything that our role models in the media are: young, beautiful and rampant. And to be young, beautiful and rampant we have to buy certain products that will make us young, beautiful and rampant. The macho culture is still very much alive today and the media continue to foster the desires of men to strut and posture and show off their power and virility. Most Hollywood films portray heroes who excel at hand-to-hand fighting and who are irresistible to women. When a man realises that his powers are waning he can become desperate. He will look for younger women because they will look up to him (whereas his wife knows his failings well); they will stimulate his flagging sexual powers and he can show them off to other men.

After a visit to his solicitor, Graham is dumbfounded. He will have to give half of everything he has worked for all his life to Sue! And all she contributed was a bit of housework and a poxy little part-time job to fill in her spare time!

A year later and Graham is a worried man. His divorce is well on the way and he has found that he will not only have to let Sue keep the house but that he will have to pay her a hefty chunk of maintenance as well. He isn't going to have much money after he has paid the rent on the house he and Michelle are living in. He is worried about his work as well. It doesn't look as though he is going to get the promotion he was expecting. Younger men seem to be overtaking him in the hierarchy. There are also rumours of a re-structuring. His job might be at risk. His boss has been making noises about early retirement. How can he be expected to keep two families on a pension? And there is no chance he will get another job at the same sort of pay he is getting, not at his age.

But what worries him most of all is that last night, for the first time ever, he failed to get an erection. He felt so embarrassed and ashamed and helpless. Michelle did her best but the old fellow just wouldn't stand up. She was quite kind about it. She did acknowledge that they had been out every night for the past week dancing and to parties. At his age he was likely to get a bit tired. 'At his age!' Oh hell! What if he could never do it again? And, to cap it all, Michelle thinks she might be pregnant. Graham doesn't know whether to be elated or desperate. His memories of the disruption caused by his children when they were babies are vague but they *have still left an impression. And Michelle isn't the old-fashioned kind of woman who will do all the nursing and housework. In fact, she is a bit careless around the house. He has even had to do some cleaning himself when somebody was coming to visit. He didn't want his friends to see what a mess they live in.*

The business world, for all its talk of keeping up to date, is slow to take on new ideas. The purpose of business is to find new and more ingenious ways of getting money out of other people's pockets into those of the shareholders and management at the lowest cost. It is still set in the macho culture, where young men are encouraged to be sharp, thrusting and ruthless. The middle-aged man no longer fits this image. He is beginning to fade and is no longer a likely candidate for promotion. Many companies try to get rid of senior managers in order to clear the path for the younger, more vigorous men to make their way to the top.

One year after the divorce Graham finds himself alone. He has been given early retirement. It was a choice of that or being made redundant. Michelle has become bored with him and left him for another of the managers at his company, one who has kept his job. Thankfully she was not pregnant. Strangely, Graham feels a sense of relief. All those nights out were exhausting him. But he is very unhappy and lonely. He seems to have become invisible to women when in his prime he would have attracted admiring glances. His children come to see him occasionally but they are still angry with him for breaking up the family. He finds he doesn't have much to say to them when they come. He never had the time to get to know them while they were children and now they seem rather distant and incomprehensible to him. He does have some male friends but their conversation revolves around cars and sport. There is little comfort in their company. He doesn't see them very often because he feels awkward not being part of a couple. So he doesn't go out very much. He finds himself sitting alone all day in his little house. He is getting very depressed and wondering what has happened to him and what point there is in living any more . . .

We have been living in a culture that is designed for the young, and both men and women have become trapped in it. But this culture is beginning to break down. Until recently it has been accepted that men should be dominant because of the necessity for them to earn money to keep their families. And until the introduction of methods of birth control women have been so occupied with child care and frequent pregnancies that they have not been able to assert themselves and have largely accepted male dominance.

The result has been that people have been forced into moulds made for them by society. Men are obliged to be strong and powerful, whether they are or not. They have been required to be able to fight, to be highly competitive, even aggressive, and to have the left-brain skills of logic, order and problem-solving. Women have had to be submissive and gentle, and to use right-brain skills which are to do with feelings, communication and relationships. So none of us have been encouraged to use all of our faculties. By mid-life most of us are only half-developed; we end up being one-sided.

In the capitalist world, too, there is little room for creativity. As James Hillman says, the existing power structure 'is fixated literally on the concrete – economics, power politics, energy, whatever – without any psychological, without any anima overtone' (Hillman, 1983). Everything has to be explained logically or by scientific experiment. Creativity and artistic talents are not valued. It is accepted that artists starve in garrets because a materialist world has no room for the imagination, except where it can be useful as advertising material or saleable as a commodity, such as a television programme or the products of an artist who has become fashionable. New ideas that conflict with the status quo are not welcomed. James Hillman goes on to say: 'We need doubt – the possibility of change. It opens it up to new ideas – new possibilities – enhancement – fluidity – why do people fear it so much?' (Hillman, 1983).

People cannot fit into moulds. Everybody is unique. Some men are gentle, some women are assertive, and everyone has a capacity for creativity of some kind. To fit into society we do our best to fit into the roles set out for us, but we can only do it for so long. There comes a time when the other aspects of our selves must be recognised, otherwise we are not complete people. By mid-life those parts of us that have been pushed into the background begin to assert themselves. If we don't allow it to happen we will come to a full stop. We will become depressed; we may become bitter and angry people. Or we will simply cease to develop and get stuck in time.

Mid-life is a time when the old models don't fit any more. Women seem to change more than men at this time. Perhaps it is because their roles have traditionally been more restricted. Nowadays, once they are released from the burdens of child-rearing they find themselves with much more energy and freedom to take on new challenges. The biological change is more marked for women too, because they go through the menopause. If they can free themselves from the old expectations that a woman's purpose in life is to bear and rear children, they find a whole new world opening up for them. Once a woman has reached the menopause she finds herself with much more energy. She is not ready yet to become old.

Men can find this very frightening and confusing. Until mid-life they have been the masters but now the ground beneath their feet begins to slip away.

Jim is a builder who works for himself. He has a couple of men who work for him but he is the boss and lets everybody know it. His work hasn't been easy, what with lazy labourers and people who won't pay their invoices, not to mention the weather holding up jobs. But he likes his work. It is satisfying to see something grow up from nothing and get finished, even if it is only a garage or an extension to somebody's house. The

What Mid-Life Crisis?

trouble is that his body is beginning to get creaky and he knows that he won't be able to shin up ladders for ever.

He is also very puzzled by his wife. She has always complained that he never did any repairs around his own house. Well, isn't that typical of all builders? But since the children have got older she is hardly in the house any more. Sometimes she isn't even there when he comes home from work. He doesn't like that. She should have his tea on the table when he comes in. And she goes out most Saturday mornings. It's this job of hers. She started working in a flower shop, just part time. He didn't mind that. There wasn't much for her to do around the house with the children grown up and she was getting bored. She seemed to like the job. But now she has started to take an interest in doing flower arrangements for weddings. And she has taken over ordering the flowers and even doing the books for the shop. He doesn't mind her doing his accounts but when she is doing somebody else's and it means that he will not get his tea made for him – that's another matter. He tried to tell her he doesn't like it but she just laughed at him! She always used to be so meek and mild. And she is earning quite a lot of money. Almost as much as he does. If he says they can't have a new TV or living room carpet – she goes ahead and buys them anyway! He's not master in his own home any more. It makes him feel like a real wuss. What's he going to do? He is frightened. If he can't be a builder any more, what will he be? His wife has become a stranger to him. What if

Men at Mid-Life

she leaves him? He doesn't want to be all alone. His life seems to be coming to a full stop . . .

Jim has fulfilled the role of a working man to perfection until now. He has worked hard, held his own in male company and been respected. But he can't keep doing those things for ever. And there doesn't seem to be a role for him any more.

Men seem to have a more difficult time at mid-life. They have been used to holding a position of superiority in the family. They have been breadwinners. In Western society a man is defined by his job. I particularly noticed, when I was married, that when we met new people they always asked my husband what he did for a living but never asked me what I did. A man without a job is deemed to be worthless. That is why so much distress is caused for men during a recession. It isn't just about earning money. Our man at mid-life has to change the way he defines himself. Even if a man has done well in life and reaches a high position in his work, by mid-life he feels that there is something missing. This is a time when he really must turn away from the expectations of society and start to take himself seriously. Men, particularly, are not used to looking at themselves and taking note of their feelings. Until now it has been OK for a man to express anger or delight at, for instance, winning a football match. But the other emotions have been forbidden. He can't express sorrow, he can't cry with joy, he can't be unsure of himself, he can't be frightened. All these feelings have to be suppressed. Well, those feelings can't stay suppressed for a lifetime. By mid-life they are beginning to leak out. But because they can't be identified they probably take the form of either anger or depression. The stress of having to keep his feelings bottled up can have severe consequences, such as high blood pressure and heart disease.

But that doesn't have to happen. A man needs to develop his other qualities. He needs to bring out his more sensitive side. If he stops taking his wife for granted or resenting her, but instead takes an interest in what she is doing and thinking and feeling, wouldn't that improve their relationship? Men are expected to be good at logic and problem-solving and practical work. Mid-life is an opportunity for a man to develop his creative qualities. He may have had interests in the past but not had the time to do anything about them. As Jung says, 'far too many aspects of life which should also have been experienced lie in the lumber-room among dusty memories. Sometimes, even, they are glowing coals under grey ashes' (Jung, 2001). A man can find satisfaction in fanning the embers of the parts of himself that he has not been allowed to bring into the open: producing a work of art, learning to play a musical instrument, cooking, gardening, photography or making something beautiful. It is an opportunity to go back to study things he never had a chance to when he was a boy. After all, his wife is probably earning as much as he is – let her keep him for a few years while he looks into those things that have always fascinated him but that he has never been given a chance to do anything about. There is no family to support any more. He is a free man, if only he will realise it.

Mid-life is a time when, freed from responsibilities, we can start to take an interest in the world around us and to reach out a helping hand to people. Many people at this age begin to do voluntary work or, if they are at work, they take on mentoring roles, helping their colleagues to learn and develop. Some people even take off and go to developing countries to give them the benefit of their knowledge and experience.

If we are going to be emotionally healthy we have to keep growing and changing. We have to learn from our experiences. And we have to carry on taking an interest in the world around us. If we get stuck we suffer.

Women at Mid-Life

Val is 48. She has been married for twenty-seven years. She met her husband David at the local factory, where he still works on the maintenance team. Their marriage has been a happy one, she thinks. Soon after they married Val became pregnant and gave up work at the factory to look after the baby. She was glad to give up the job and she loved being at home with the child. She was a very loving mother and doted on the child. Two more children followed and her whole life was taken up with caring for them. She was at her happiest when the children were small, needing so much attention. When they reached their teens they were a bit difficult, but no more than normal teenagers. They began to spend more and more time with their own friends and did not need her so much. To pass the time she got a part-time job in a shop, which she quite enjoyed, chatting to the other women employees. The money she earned was usually spent on things for the house and clothes for the children. She loved cooking and making dinners for the family.

    Now things are changing for Val. Her youngest child is moving out to live with her boyfriend. The house is empty. There is only her and David to make it dirty so there is hardly any housework. She is beginning to feel lonely and useless. She misses all the clamour of a lively family. And, to cap it all, she thinks she is in the

What Mid-Life Crisis?

'change'. She has started missing periods and sometimes at night she gets so hot! She is turning into an old woman! No chance of any more babies. What is the point of her life now?

The impact of reaching mid-life is more defined for women. We go through the menopause. It is a demarcation line between our lives as mothers and . . . what?

Many women feel anxious at this time. Their role in life has been fulfilled, they have brought up a family, there doesn't seem to be anything more to do. But this is also a time when women can begin to enjoy freedom. They are free from family duties and, after many years of putting everyone else first, can start to think about themselves and what *they* want in life. Most women have not had an opportunity to establish a career because the needs of the family have come first. This is changing, gradually, but for most people who have reached this stage in life it was always the man's career that was paramount and everything else was geared to help him to earn more money. Women, on the other hand, have traditionally been given the more nurturing work of caring for children, protecting them, helping them to grow, listening to their concerns. Their creativeness has usually been constrained by the needs of their families while they are growing up. There has been little time for hobbies or opportunities to try new things.

A woman's place has traditionally been in the home. This tradition is gradually changing, but for most women who are now reaching mid-life the expectation has been that they were in charge of the house and the children. They were not expected to have careers outside the home but they could take part-time jobs to help with the family budget. However, their main occupation was to look after their husband and children. They were expected to deal with emotional issues and look after the well being of the family, while the husband brought in the money to keep them. Women became skilled at being caring, nurturing wives and mothers. For many women this was a fulfilling life and they were happy to be caregivers. The difficulty comes when the children leave the home and there is no family left to care for. The menopause means the end of fertility, which has been very important in a woman's life, defining her purpose as a mother and caregiver. At mid-life all those skills of multi-tasking – keeping house, quelling squabbles, organising school uniforms, lunches, bus fares, looking after the emotional needs of her children, giving love – become redundant. If a woman defines herself around these tasks she is in danger of becoming seriously depressed at mid-life.

But women, if they can come to terms with the loss of their ability to have children, have an advantage over men at mid-life.

Rose is 55. She was married to Mike for thirty-five years until she left him last year. It did seem a pity to break up such a long marriage. It wasn't really an unhappy one. They rubbed along together all right but their lives had become so dull. And she is angry. She doesn't really blame Mike but she still feels angry. It

What Mid-Life Crisis?

was OK when they first got married. The children came along and she was kept busy with them. Mike didn't have much to do with the children: it was always left to her to look after them when they were ill or upset. In fact, once the children were born, he just seemed to drift away from them as a family. He went to work, came home, watched television. They didn't go out much – they were pretty strapped for cash for a long time.

Rose thought she probably started getting angry when she joined the art club. She had gone to an evening class with her friend, Jenny, just to keep her company. She found the class absolutely fascinating. The time passed so quickly and she produced some pretty good drawings and paintings for a beginner. So she joined the local art society and went out with them on a Saturday afternoon, painting in the open air. They were a nice bunch of people and she really enjoyed her Saturday afternoons. But Mike soon put a stop to that. He got fed up with having to make tea for their two boys. When she came home he would give her the silent treatment. He would sulk all weekend. In the end she had given up doing the art. It was all too much trouble.

Then, when the children got older, Rose started working part time in the local factory. It was just for a bit of pin money and to get her out of the house for a bit. Well, the boss soon started to notice her. It was obvious that he fancied her but she didn't encourage him. As well as that, he realised how bright she was and he began giving her more responsible jobs to do. He *eventually offered her the job of Factory Manager. Fancy that! Her just a housewife! Of course Mike wouldn't have it. He didn't want her coming home late every night. It would mean they didn't get their tea until about seven o'clock by the time she had come home and cooked it. So Rose packed in that job and took one instead at a nearby packing warehouse. The same thing happened again. She started part time and ended up running the place. This time she didn't listen to Mike. He had to wait for his tea until she came home. In the end it dawned on her that she didn't really need Mike at all. It was just a chore having to cook every night, whether she wanted a big meal or not. She was fed up with cleaning up after him. He didn't even notice all the work she did in the house, even though they were both out at work full time. They didn't have much to say to one another any more. They just sort of put up with each other. And she felt like taking up painting again.*

So now Rose is living in a flat on her own. She finds it wonderful to have the freedom to eat when she wants, watch what she wants on TV, go out when she wants. She has made lots of friends at work and at the artists' club she has re-joined. She revels in spending weekends lost in her painting. There is a nice man at the club, too, nothing much to look at but he seems interested in her and he has suggested that they might go round some art galleries together. She might not be over the hill after all. But she isn't going to get married again. She enjoys living by herself far too much . . .

What Mid-Life Crisis?

Rose was happy to fit into the role of housewife and mother at first but then she started to outgrow the mould. She had a creative side that was demanding to be developed but was not allowed to. She was bright and clever, which was soon recognised by her employers. She got satisfaction out of doing a demanding job and that eventually took priority over Mike's desire that she be always available to minister to his needs. Their relationship became stale because they took each other for granted. They ceased to communicate. Eventually Rose realised that her energies and desire for stimulation and her wish to develop her creative talents were being squashed. She had to release herself from the marriage and she was much happier living by herself.

For women who have not had children there are different issues. They may not have been able to have children for health or biological reasons; maybe their circumstances did not allow it; maybe they chose to pursue their careers rather than have children. Now it is time for these women to come to terms with their loss, perhaps to grieve. Grieving is a task; it is a process that has to be gone through. It is important not to try to suppress it but to feel the sadness and anger, although we should take care not to get stuck in the grieving process. There will be a time when the pain is still there to some extent, but we can begin to look forward to enjoying the rest of our lives.

Menopause

> You spend the first half of your adult life trying not to get pregnant; then you spend the second half trying to get knocked up. (Sheehy, 1995)

The change of life is so much more marked for a woman. A baby girl is born with a store of eggs in her ovaries. At puberty, when the womb is ready, one egg will descend into the fallopian tube and then down into the womb. If it is fertilised by a sperm it will stay and form a baby. If it is not fertilised it will be flushed away, along with the lining of the womb, which is what we term as a period. This happens every month until, at about the age of 50, all the eggs are used up. The woman is no longer able to produce children (unless she can persuade an expensive doctor to implant a fertilised egg into her womb).

After the age of 40 it is much more difficult for women to conceive. And there is increasing danger that the baby will not be healthy. This is because the eggs in a woman's ovaries can begin to deteriorate with time. A lot of women are helped today by in vitro fertilisation (IVF), where the sperm is introduced directly into the egg, rather than making its normal way via the vagina. This process involves many intrusive medical procedures and can cost a lot of money. And it isn't always successful. Many women today are postponing having children until they are firmly embarked on their careers but this can have tragic consequences if they leave it too late.

What Mid-Life Crisis?

The menopause produces many symptoms, most of which happen during pre-menopause. These start, usually, at about the age of 40. The effects of the pre-menopause symptoms vary with individual women. Some women suffer badly, while others have very little trouble at all. In this male-dominated society it is not a subject that has been studied thoroughly and many women still find it embarrassing to talk to their partners about it. They therefore usually suffer in silence.

Some of the features of pre-menopause are depression, headaches, tiredness, mood swings, a decrease in sexual response and, most common of all, lapses of memory and hot flushes.

It is not clear whether depression at this time is caused by hormonal changes or by the feelings of loss of fertility. In many cultures today, and even in the West, a woman's duty is to bear and rear children. At menopause a woman can feel that she is no longer a woman; she has become a useless old hag. Her self-esteem drops and she becomes very unhappy.

During the years before menopause the monthly cycle often becomes more erratic. Sometimes periods may be missed and at other times women suffer from more frequent periods or excessive bleeding. The latter happens because in the months when ovulation does not occur a woman produces no progesterone – the hormone ordinarily responsible for flushing the lining of the uterus. The endometrial lining becomes thicker and may not be entirely discarded until the next cycle, when the body rids itself of the build-up (Sheehy, 1991). Excessive bleeding often leads to women having unnecessary hysterectomy operations.

Older women can also suffer from endometriosis. This is where cells like the ones found in the womb lining grow on organs outside the womb. These go through the same monthly changes as the womb lining itself, sometimes swelling and bleeding into the body cavity. This bleeding can cause pain and swelling because, unlike a normal monthly period, the blood from endometriosis can't escape from the body through the vagina. Instead, the blood stays inside the body and may form rubbery bands of scar tissue, called adhesions. These can attach organs and tissues together and affect organs surrounding the womb (see BUPA's fact sheet: www.bupa.co.uk). They can also cause bladder problems. The symptoms of endometriosis usually disappear after menopause.

At this time a woman's body begins to produce less oestrogen, the female hormone. This can have several effects. Lack of oestrogen is the cause of the distressing lapses of memory that women experience in later life. It can also lead to the bone disease osteoporosis where bones become brittle and start to crumble and break. It leads to dryness and thinning of the walls of the vagina. Sex can be painful and cause tearing and bleeding. There can also be an increase in cystitis and candida infections.

All of these symptoms can be alleviated by hormone replacement therapy (HRT). But this can have many side-effects which affect women differently. The advice of a doctor should be sought before embarking on HRT.

What Mid-Life Crisis?

    The effects of all these hormonal and bodily changes can leave a woman tired and irritable. They also lead to disturbed sleep and insomnia which, in turn, can affect a woman's health.

    However, once menopause has been reached, usually about the age of 50, most of the unpleasant symptoms, such as hot flushes, swelling and bladder problems, disappear. One result of having less of the female hormone oestrogen is that it can make women more masculine in their behaviour. They become more assertive and stronger. They are also much more vigorous. So they come out of menopause full of life and ready for anything. They are ready to take on new challenges, to throw off their old patterns of duty and submissiveness and enjoy their lives. Post-menopause a woman's sexuality is highly charged. She can be capable of many orgasms, one after another. Unfortunately, this is just at the time when her partner's sexual performance is beginning to falter. In fact there can be a role reversal. Mid-life women can be very predatory. They search for sex and for different partners. A man may be led on by a mid-life woman and then dropped. It may make him feel used and put him off women.

Marriage and Partnerships

Gone are the days when people are expected to get married before they are 25. But for those of us born in the baby boom generation of the 1950s and 1960s, that was not the case. If we were not married by 25 people thought there was something wrong with us. Very often we chose the first reasonable person who came along. Many were forced to marry because of pregnancy as it was considered sinful for a baby to be born out of wedlock. Homosexuals and lesbians were obliged to hide their sexuality by getting married.

In those days we were trapped in the traditional roles. The man was the breadwinner and the woman looked after the home and the children. The old patterns of life don't work any more. Women are no longer content to stay at home. But they don't have the same support structures as men. Things are changing slowly, but there is still not the same expectation for women to find careers. They have to fit jobs and careers around child care. And, more often than not, they still have to take responsibility for the housekeeping. Both partners work extremely hard and are under pressure. The man has to keep his position at work and his social standing, and the woman has to juggle work and domestic responsibilities. They have to keep up with the demands of their children for the latest electronic toys and designer clothes and the expectation that they should have a

What Mid-Life Crisis?

house furnished in the latest style and have expensive foreign holidays.

It is no wonder that marriages and partnerships fail to thrive under these pressures. The pace of life is so frenetic that couples don't have any time to spend bonding with their partner or their children. Usually, when they do have some time to spare, it is spent slumped in front of the television in a state of exhaustion. Often one or both of them will be forced to work a lot of overtime to make ends meet, or because it is expected of them by the culture at their workplace. The result is that the family loses the chance to communicate. Meals are scraped together in a hurry and eaten in front of the television. The couple become strangers to one another. Dissatisfactions and resentments are not dealt with and they begin to fester. By mid-life it may be too late to retrieve the love and harmony they had when first embarking on marriage. Small hurts can result in silence and withdrawal, which then could be seen as hostility by the other partner and result in anger and aggression. Or they can lead to quarrels which go round and round, with both partners saying the same things and neither listening to the other.

When things go wrong it is easy to blame our partner instead of examining our own part in what has happened. If we put all our problems onto someone else we don't have to take responsibility, we don't have to look inside ourselves and we don't have to change. Eventually we can come to believe that by leaving our partner we are leaving all our problems behind. Very often we will find that if we do leave our partner and start a relationship with somebody else the same problems arise with the new partner. We have to take a hard look at ourselves and at what is driving us, because if we don't change ourselves and how we behave we will keep going round the same patterns again and again. This often happens with women who are battered or abused in other ways by their partners. So often they will eventually leave this partner, only to find themselves in the same situation with someone else. Unfortunately it is the job of the woman herself to look at her past, deal with her hurts, become more assertive and recover her self-esteem so that she will not continue to attract partners who will abuse her.

The traditional form of marriage has led to the husband expecting his wife to take over from his mother, protecting and nurturing him. His wife will expect him to take over the role of her father, protecting and providing. But there is bound to be a time when they are both matured: the man no longer wants to be mothered or the woman to be protected and kept. If either partner tries to stay in their traditional roles they will find their mate becoming more and more exasperated with them.

When the job of rearing the children is allocated to the wife, she learns about feelings and emotions. She learns to deal with the problems that beset her children. It is she who finds out that they are being bullied at school and does her best to try to deal with it. She has to cope when the children are ill, trying somehow to look after them and keep her job at the same time. She is usually the one who keeps up with family birthdays and anniversaries. She gets involved with family squabbles and feuds. She deals with difficult issues such as death in the family and other tragedies. She does all this, usually, from a position of powerlessness. Unless she has a high-power job she has no status in society. So she learns to cope with difficulties when they arise and it helps her to be resilient. The traditional husband, on the other hand, keeps his distance from family troubles, leaving his wife to cope. As a result the wife becomes emotionally strong and capable, whereas her husband has had little or no experience of dealing with emotional issues. She becomes mature, whereas he stays immature. The result is that the two become incompatible.

Mid-life is a dangerous time for relationships. When the children start to need less nurturing and are becoming more independent, the wife's attention turns to life outside the home. After the exhausting business of bringing up children she now finds herself with energy to spare. She may pay more attention to her job and take on more responsibility or take up a career that has been on hold for many years. She may embark on a new career altogether or go back to college. At the same time her partner is beginning to get tired of the rat race and to look inwards to home and to developing those nurturing qualities that he has previously lacked, only to find that his wife's attention is taken up with her own interests and career. He feels sidelined, hurt and neglected. Until now all the focus has been upon him. He may wonder why what he has always provided isn't good enough any more. It may make him feel inadequate and rejected. The traditional roles are reversed. She is becoming more assertive

Marriage and Partnerships

and no longer asks his permission to do things. She is earning her own money. While he is trying to get her attention she may feel that he is trying to control her. She may be clumsy in the way she uses her new-found assertiveness and he may see it as aggression.

Each partner must allow things to change. We are individuals. If we are to be fully developed human beings we have to be given room to change. Our partner must give us space to try new things, to branch out on our own. Otherwise there is the danger that we will walk away. As James Hollis says in *The Middle Passage*:

> If a spouse feels threatened by change, and resists, then he or she can be assured of living with an angry and depressed partner ... change will be inevitable. Otherwise the marriage may not survive, especially if it hinders the growth of either partner. (Hollis, 1993)

If couples do not allow for change to take place they will find themselves living a very one-dimensional life. Neither of them has allowed themselves to develop, to become fully rounded characters. They are stuck in narrow roles, left behind by the rest of society. If the relationship is built around the man's achievements outside the home, then what happens if he loses his job or is made to retire early? He will lose his identity, and his wife, who has always had her identity bound up with his, will be left with nothing (Sheehy, 1976). Couples who keep the old roles can also run into trouble if the wife begins to resent the husband's assumption of authority. Or the woman can give up any responsibility for herself, become the victim and blame all her ills on her man. As long as she continues to do that she doesn't have to change.

The dilemma is that if the wife does start to change, her husband may not like like it when she starts to assert herself. On the other hand, if she stays dependent and doesn't change he may get fed up and leave her. Women may become dissatisfied with a partner who insists on being dominant. However, there is no reason why she would not be happy if he becomes more emotionally mature.

The unfortunate need for many men to live a macho lifestyle can have a damaging effect on their relationships. While they are busy posturing, fighting, jockeying for position as dominant male, showing off their strength and virility, their wives are quietly becoming more mature. They find this teenage behaviour irritating. Men need to learn to stop seeing women as objects. If they can't do that they will never be able to have successful, fulfilling relationships. And what happens when the man starts to lose his strength and virility? In his own mind he feels worthless.

Another problem for couples in modern society is that it is easy for them to spend all their time together, to the exclusion of friends and interests outside the family. It is seen so often when a young couple get together. They let their friends go, especially friends of the opposite sex. When the partnership gets rocky there is nobody else to support them, especially as they move around in search of work and lose the ties of family, friends and neighbours nearby.

Mid-life is a time when we begin to look towards the future. We realise that the time we have left is limited. We have to make sense of our past and decide what we want to keep in our lives and what we need to shed. One of those things may be the hectic pace of modern life. There is often a need to spend more time in quiet and solitude to think things through and come to terms with life. This drastic change in our lifestyle may puzzle or alarm our partners. They may feel neglected or sidelined. We need to make sure to tell them that we still love them but that we need this space apart for our own peace of mind.

Sex and Our Bodies

> When two people are under the influence of the most violent, most insane, most delusive and most transient of passions, they are required to swear that they will remain in that excited, abnormal, and exhausting condition continuously until death do them part. (G. B. Shaw)

> ... desire can only survive in lack. In fulfilment it collapses. (Freud, 1912)

These two quotations sum up the problem with sex. Yes, it is wonderful and exciting with a new partner but after a while there is the danger that it can become stale. When the first passion starts to settle down the impetus gets lost.

What Mid-Life Crisis?

When the couple inevitably start to have disagreements, if these are not dealt with in a sensitive and caring way they can fester and lead to disenchantment, dislike, distance. Their sex life is bound to suffer.

At mid-life men often go after younger women and women go after younger men. They feel that they may have missed out on experiences they could have had; they are beginning to get old and this may be their last chance to go out and have a good time. Men may need to prove their male prowess before they lose it altogether. Once their libido starts to slow down they can find themselves invigorated by a new, younger partner. Traditionally women have been expected to hide their sexuality for fear of being considered 'loose'. By mid-life women want to get rid of those restraints, break out and enjoy sex to the full. Older women are not likely to settle down into a permanent relationship with a younger male partner. They are more likely to be enjoying the freedom of having a lover. On the other hand, a man will marry a much younger woman but then life can get very difficult for him. He has finished with babies and children in his former marriage and now he has to start all over again. His libido may have been re-awakened by his new partner but once the passion is over his sexual problems start all over again. What he really needs is more time on his own to learn about himself. A relationship with a much younger woman won't bring him that. It will just delay his maturity.

Another reason why men go for younger girls is that mature women frighten them. They are too knowing and experienced. They expect too much.

Marriage and Partnerships

In the modern world sex is everywhere. We can't get away from it. If we use such and such a shampoo we will be irresistible to the opposite sex. If we own certain products we will attract lots of nubile young women. There is so much media attention given to film and television stars. Are we all expected to look and behave like them? If that is the case, then it is not surprising that so many marriages and partnerships fail. If people take celebrities as their role models they will find that shallow relationships with unsuitable partners do not lead to a satisfying and fulfilled life. Eventually, with a bit of maturity people realise that they can't act like teenagers all their lives. They need to look at other ways of behaving.

On top of all these common problems around sex and partnerships there eventually come the problems associated with ageing. There is a change in hormone balance in both men and women. Oestrogen drops in women, testosterone drops in men over 50, but they always have ten times more testosterone than females (Sheehy, 1995).

A man reaches his peak of sexual performance when he is about 17 years old. After that his (so-called) performance goes down. This is borne out by figures from Gail Sheehy's book *New Passages*. The Massachusetts Male Aging Study 1993 states that 'About half of American men over 40 have experienced middle-life impotence to varying degrees', and a MORI poll in England in 1993 stated that 'Nearly a third of all British men over the age of 50 do not have sexual intercourse. Even among men who were still sexually active, almost half complained of poor erections since they had turned 50' (Sheehy, 1995).

In a world where sexual performance is given such importance this can be disastrous for a man. If his whole sense of self is centred around his masculinity he is in trouble. The first time he fails to perform can be very frightening for him. For a man who is used to being able to produce an erection almost at the drop of a hat (or other item of clothing) this is a disaster. In fact there is no reason why people cannot perform and enjoy a satisfactory sex life well into their old age. At 50 a man may take longer to come to ejaculation and have to wait several hours after ejaculation before he can do it again. This is good news for women. Long and slow is much more satisfying for them.

There are many reasons why men suffer from impotence at middle age. One of the main reasons is that their confidence goes. A lot of men suffer from an all-or-nothing way of thinking. A man may think that if he has failed to perform once he will never be able to do it again. And so, next time he wants to have sex all he can think about is failure. Our subconscious is very obedient. Think about failure and the subconscious will bring it about.

Or he may think that older people can't have sex and that he is doomed to a sexless life from now on. For those of us who grew up in the 1950s and early 1960s sex, and especially the sexuality of our parents, was hidden from us. We believed that our parents did not 'do it'. That may not have been the case for those who grew up in the

Marriage and Partnerships

1970s, but most young people still think that the idea of older people engaging in sex is 'gross'. Well, they will just have to get used to the idea that lots of people go on to enjoy sex well into their seventies and eighties.

Another psychological reason for loss of libido is depression. This takes away a person's enjoyment of life and stops him or her from even thinking about engaging in a loving relationship. Depression keeps us in a flat and meaningless existence without any interest in life. It can be an escape from the world and the pain that can be caused by our relationships with other people.

Loss of status can affect a man's self-confidence. If he loses his job or has a setback in his career it can affect his sexual performance.

There are also physical reasons why men become impotent. The build-up of cholesterol can line the blood vessels, thus preventing the blood from engorging the penis. This can be caused by smoking, lack of exercise and a fatty diet. Bad diet can also lead to diabetes, which affects the circulation and prevents men from being able to achieve erections.

Stress alone can be a cause of impotence. It causes the blood vessels to constrict so that the penis cannot become engorged (Sheehy, 1995). Stress can also cause both cholesterol build-up and high blood pressure, putting a strain on the heart and on the rest of the body. And a lot of men and women work too hard – no wonder they haven't the energy to perform sexually.

A man's body does change with age. He will start losing muscle and gaining body fat. The changes in his hormone balance can bring on symptoms ranging from broken sleep, lethargy and depression to irritability, nervousness, trouble concentrating, memory lapses and mood swings (Sheehy, 1995). Women also suffer from similar symptoms when they go through the menopause.

The tragedy is that in today's culture, while women will discuss their problems with their doctor or close friends, most men find it impossible to confess their sexual or emotional difficulties to anybody. A man will not even consult his doctor for fear of being seen to lose image and status. With a little help many of these problems could be overcome quite easily. And there is always Viagra and similar drugs which can help with erection problems (Viagra relaxes the linings of the blood vessels, allowing the penis to become engorged).

Couples should make an effort to revitalise their sex life. There are any number of books and videos on how to do that. Men, particularly, need look after their physical health and strength and work on expanding the intimacy in their marriages. If they can do this it is unlikely that they will have potency problems (Sheehy, 1995). Now is the time to ignore all the old taboos about sex, to talk to our partners and experiment.

Sex at mid-life can be so satisfying. It is about caring for and pleasuring the other, being intimate. While a man may not be able to ejaculate more than once in a few hours, he can learn to draw out the pleasure, to introduce humour, to take breaks. His partner is capable of many orgasms, one after another, and he can enjoy giving her that pleasure. If he saves up his orgasm, even until the next time they have sex, when it comes it will be all the more explosive.

But intimacy is more important than sex at this time of life. Couples can have very pleasurable, relaxed, intimate, fulfilled relationships at this time and come closer to each other than they ever were before.

Of course, if we are to enjoy the second half of our lives it is important to stay fit and well. We have to make sure we have a varied and healthy diet and get plenty of exercise, especially if we intend to continue to enjoy sex well into our old age. We also have to think about giving up smoking and reducing our intake of alcohol or other drugs if we want to last long enough to enjoy the most pleasurable and comfortable part of our lives.

Enhancing Relationships at Mid-Life

> You were born together, and together you shall be for evermore.
> You shall be together when the white wings of death scatter your days.
> Aye, you shall be together even in the silent memory of God.
> But let there be spaces in your togetherness.
> And let the winds of the heavens dance between you.
>
> Love one another, but make not a bond of love:
> Let it rather be a moving sea between the shores of your souls.
> Fill each other's cup but drink not from one cup.

What Mid-Life Crisis?

Give one another of your bread but eat not from the same loaf.
Sing and dance together and be joyous, but let each one of you be alone,
Even as the strings of a lute are alone although they quiver with the same music.

Give your hearts, but not into each other's keeping
For only the hand of Life can contain your hearts.
And stand together yet not too near together:
For the pillars of the temple stand apart,
And the oak tree and the cypress grow not in each other's shadow.
(Kahlil Gibran, The Prophet)

Above all we have achieved a real independence and with it, to be sure, a certain isolation. In a sense we are alone, for our 'inner freedom' means that a love relation can no longer fetter us; the other sex has lost its magic power over us . . . We shall not easily 'fall in love', for we can no longer lose ourselves in someone else, but we shall be capable of a deeper love, a conscious devotion to the other. (Jung, 1973)

At mid-life we are forced to start looking at ourselves – at who we really are, rather than the role we have been thrust into by society. We need to develop the undeveloped parts of ourselves, to become fully rounded human beings. We need to start exploring the things that have always intrigued us but that we never had the time to

Marriage and Partnerships

pursue. We need to involve ourselves in the arts, or travelling, or literature, or starting a new business or climbing mountains or spirituality, anything that interests us. And we must allow our partners to do the same. We have to put up with their long absences, with their being distracted, and get on with our own interests. We have to allow them to change their priorities, to lose interest in money and position. We can't expect their full and undivided attention at all times and they should not expect ours. This is a time when we have to grow up and learn to live life independently. We have to learn not to rely on someone else to complete us. If we are secure within ourselves we are better able to give to another without endangering our sense of self.

We can't expect, either, to ditch our partner in order to look for someone else who will look after us and care for us and provide all those things we don't have ourselves. That person does not exist. We have to learn to be independent, to rely on ourselves. If your spouse has gone off on such a search, it may be worthwhile just to sit tight and wait until they return. However, it is likely that by the time they do return you have learned independence yourself and may not be willing to take them back.

Many relationships fail because people grow and develop at different rates. If you feel your partner is growing away from you, are you willing to change what you do and how you think? After all, taking small risks and making changes now can prevent the calamity of losing your partner altogether. People must talk to their partners – try to understand how the other feels. Look at your partner – how can you enhance your relationship? Are you taking him or her for granted? How can you make it better? Why don't you ask them?

If you are worried about the impact your growth and development may have on your partner it is important to remember that only by living your own life clearly can you free up your partner to grow and develop in their own way.

Being Single Again

> There's this primary America of freeways and jet flights and TV and movie spectaculars. And people caught up in this primary America seem to go through huge portions of their lives without much consciousness of what's immediately around them. The Media have convinced them that what's right around them is unimportant. And that's why they're lonely . . . You're not what they're looking for. You're not on TV. (Pirsig, 1974)

I am sure that many of us chose to marry the first reasonable person who came along, because we were afraid of being left 'on the shelf'. However, many of us have found ourselves back on the shelf for periods of time. But, as we are finding out, our shelf life is much longer than anyone expected.

So what do you do when you get left by yourself? When your partner walks out? The mistake is to think that you have chosen for ever. You may be scarred and damaged

Marriage and Partnerships

but you can heal your mind and emotions. You can put it behind you and move on. You have the rest of your life to live and you can enjoy it.

Until now we have had our fathers and mothers to lean on and then our partners. At mid-life we learn that we are essentially alone. We can't rely on others to give us what we want: we must learn to achieve it for ourselves. We have to stop being dependent and learn to stand on our own two feet.

Being single again at mid-life is very different from being single as a teenager. For one thing, we have become invisible. We have lost our youth and beauty, we no longer get that second look. Even with expensive cosmetic surgery we can never recover that bloom of youth we once had. But this is no bad thing. Beautiful women often suffer for their beauty because men want to possess them, to show them off, without valuing the person they are beneath the skin. Now, when we are looking for a partner we have to look for other indicators, such as a kind face, sparkling eyes, graceful movements, pleasant manners. We are looking for the person behind the face and body, at what they are *really* like rather than just their appearance. What a departure from all that emphasis on youth and beauty! At last the less attractive of us can have our turn. The field is equal for once for those of us who weren't blessed with good looks. Now we are looking inwards at ourselves and our own growth, and we are also looking for the inner workings in those we meet instead of at the outer shell. We are much wiser and less likely to fall for someone unsuitable. Another difference

What Mid-Life Crisis?

is that most of us have our own homes, we are independent, so we are not looking for someone to keep us or look after us. We can enter a relationship on our own terms.

Remember Graham's wife, Sue, at the beginning of this book?

Sue was astounded when Graham suddenly announced that he was leaving her for Michelle, one of the receptionists at his work. She had had no idea that there was anything going on behind her back. They had become so distant from each other over the years, what with the long hours Graham put in at work. When he came home he didn't have much to say, he just sat and watched the television and grumbled at the children. It was she who had brought up the children, keeping them out of his way when he was at home. It hadn't been easy, especially when they were going through their rebellious teenage years. It was a wonder that one of them hadn't ended up in trouble with the police. She hadn't told Graham much about what was going on. He would only have got furious and maybe made things worse. Anyway, he had hardly been there most of the time. Things had got a bit easier lately and she had taken a part-time job in the office of a local firm. It gave her something to do when the children were at school and it was interesting. The firm had not been in business long but it was very successful and her work was contributing to the success.

After a few days of being completely stunned by Graham's departure Sue began to feel angry. Very

Marriage and Partnerships

angry. *How could he go swanning off with a bit of a girl! How stupid did he look posing around in his new sports car! What about his responsibilities!*

And then, as the enormity of what Graham had done began to sink in, Sue felt very vulnerable. What was she going to do? Graham had told her to move out of the house. Where were she and the children going to live? He couldn't just throw them out onto the street, could he? She felt so stupid and ashamed. What had she done to deserve this? She had been a good wife and mother. One of the women at her work advised her to consult a solicitor. Her solicitor was very encouraging. She told her that Graham could not make her move out of the house if she didn't want to and that he would have to pay her maintenance. She even had a chuckle to herself when she thought of Graham's reaction when he realised this.

After a few months Sue began to get her life back together. The amount of maintenance Graham was paying her was much less than she had been used to so she started working full-time. The boss even gave her a salary increase because he realised that she would be a valuable worker now that she was there all the time. She didn't even mind doing a little overtime when they were stretched. The confidence he had in her and the extra responsibility he was giving her made her feel much better about herself.

Some time later the children, who had kept in touch with Graham, told her that he was in a terrible state of depression. He had lost Michelle and his job. He couldn't afford to keep himself. Sue felt sorry for him but there was little she could do to help him. She didn't want him back. She had been made a partner in her firm and she had met a nice man at a singles club who wanted to marry her. But by now she had got used to being her own mistress. She appreciated having space to do what she wanted after all those years of running around after Graham. So she was quite happy having her boyfriend as a weekend lover. The children were almost independent now. Sue eventually sold the house so that Graham could have his half-share to get him back on his feet again. She bought a smaller place for herself and her youngest child.

Look at what happens to our middle-aged woman when her relationship crashes! She suddenly finds herself abandoned. Life has taught her to expect to be looked after, first by her parents and then by her husband. She may not have had responsibility for paying bills, having the car fixed, getting jobs done on the house. Now she may not even have a house. That might have been sold in the divorce settlement. This may seem disastrous but it is the best thing that can happen to her. Instead of allowing other people to look after her for the rest of her life she is forced to become independent, to develop those parts of herself that have been allowed to remain dormant. First of all she has to find somewhere to live – on her own. What a big step! But she can find something to suit herself: it may not be as grand as what she had, but at least she has a choice.

Marriage and Partnerships

Next she has to find work. It is such a pity that many women aren't able to keep up with their careers, that they have to let them slide to make time for family. She will now be much further down the ladder than people who have not had other responsibilities. But at least she can learn to keep herself. It is not necessary to have a mate. It is possible to be responsible for oneself. And now there is nothing to stop her from putting in more effort and time at work. She can get stuck into it, prove that she can take responsibility and gain promotion. She has much more reason to impress the bosses. This helps her to become more confident and assertive. She has to be assertive now that she has to fight her own battles.

This is the time to look at herself, at her appearance. If she wants a new partner she might have to smarten herself up. She can lose weight, buy more attractive clothes, learn to flirt again. After all, if she is daring enough, there are all those hundreds of men in singles clubs and on the internet looking for new partners. It is a new lease of life for our ditched wife. She becomes a different person altogether: poised, confident, independent, attractive.

Many mid-life women who are divorced choose to live alone and take lovers, rather than to marry again. Having tasted freedom they are tired of being servants and unwilling to take on the role of wife again. That does not seem to be the case for men. They want to get married again, probably because they are used to being waited upon. The complete freedom is so intoxicating that most women never want to go back to sharing a house with somebody else. They will take a lover but they will make sure that he doesn't invade her space more than she wishes. She will see him at his place or only at weekends. And she won't get involved in doing his laundry or cleaning up after him.

A single woman at mid-life has the best of both worlds. Meeting new people will help her to develop her social skills and expand her horizons. New lovers will excite her. She can explore her sexuality. Middle-aged women, once the grind of early life is over, have a rejuvenation of their libido. If they take exercise and keep fit they can enjoy a satisfying sex life until their seventies or eighties.

Mid-life men often have a more difficult time when they find themselves left on their own. Most men have been used to having someone to run around after them, listen to them, clean up after them, cook for them. Suddenly they find themselves helpless. It is a great shock, not only because there is nobody to look after them but because it is a blow to their male esteem. They have failed to keep their woman. They now have to learn to woo women once again, to take an interest in them, to learn to be caring and gentle. An older woman looking for a permanent partner is interested in more than sex – a lover is easy to find. But she wants someone who will be able to share her joys and sorrows, to be affectionate and caring, someone who will give her room to grow.

Depression and Breakdown

Jane Polden, in her excellent book on mid-life, *Regeneration*, says:

> We live in a world which idealizes competence and control and which encourages us to be compulsively extrovert and achievement orientated. But these strategies can be defences against . . . pain and loss . . . Even when anxiety – or exhaustion – does overwhelm us and bring us to a standstill, we are most unlikely to respond to it with compassion for ourselves, or even attention.

She goes on to say:

> We believe it is wrong, pointless and yet shameful to suffer pain: we should control or suppress it, and this is the aim of most psychiatric practice. We have failed in our duty to be happy and successful – or at the very least to present ourselves that way, however awful we feel inside. Shame stops us from seeking help. Death itself sometimes seems preferable. (Polden, 2002)

A nervous breakdown can take many forms but the effect is that the person withdraws from everyday life in some way. They may cease to function and have to be hospitalised, they may find themselves unable to leave the house, they may act in bizarre ways, they may take to drugs or alcohol. These are all ways that the person has found to escape from a world that has become too difficult for them to cope with. Many people retreat into fragility and become the sort of person that everybody hides unpleasantness from. The families of these people will not share with them what is really going on because they think they will not be able to cope with the reality. But then these people are not living in real life. So much is hidden from them.

Depression is often a reaction to loss – of a relationship, of a career, of possessions. It is also a way of avoiding the realities of life. It is a withdrawal from life's activities. It brings us to a full stop. We can't move on until we face up to whatever it is that has made us so unhappy. But, as Jane Polden says, 'When we are so accustomed ... to think of depression in terms of pathology and failure, it takes a great shift to begin to think about it instead as a potential turning point in the journey through life' (Polden, 2002).

Sooner or later life will throw difficulties at us. We can ignore them and carry on with our lives. It is when we receive too many blows that we cannot continue to bury our problems. As Jane Polden says, 'This is what can happen at mid-life. We can only successfully keep the unpleasant stuff under wraps, hidden from ourselves and everybody else, for so long. There comes a time when we have to deal with it' (Polden, 2002). We have to face up to what has happened to us. If we don't, our body or mind will call a halt. We may become physically ill or have a breakdown of some kind. But illness, a breakdown

Depression and Breakdown

or a period of depression does not have to be a bad thing. Our body or our mind is forcing us to stop. To have carried on in the way we were going would have destroyed us. We need time to come to terms with what has been happening and make changes. Going back to our old ways will only make us ill again. It brings to mind the phrase that kept cropping up in old Western films: 'You're running away from yourself.' It is true that sooner or later we have to face up to all that hurt we have been hiding from.

The stress of modern life and the efforts we make to keep our unhappiness hidden makes us physically ill. We suffer from high blood pressure and heart disease. Our immune system doesn't work properly and we start to get other illnesses that we would normally be able to resist.

Mid-life is a time when we are forced to look at ourselves. At some time we have to pay attention to what is going on inside. Wounds to our feelings are very much like wounds to our bodies. Some wounds are so bad that you can't just slap on a plaster and expect them to get better. If they are left to fester they can get so toxic they can poison our whole lives. They need care and attention. All the old hurts need addressing (or dressing), sometimes with the help of a professional counsellor or psychotherapist, to enable them to heal so that we will be in good shape to go on to the second phase of our lives.

These old hurts can take many forms. It is amazing how the wounds we receive in childhood can remain with us until old age if we do not pay attention to them. Have you noticed how sometimes something quite small can

What Mid-Life Crisis?

upset us so much that it is quite out of proportion? It only needs to be a word or a look or finding ourselves in a certain situation. Very often if we sit and think about it, we can find that the present situation somehow reminds us of a time in the past when we were very hurt. It could go back a long way. We need to find the courage to look back at what happened and try to deal with it.

Guilt and Shame

Carrying around guilt and shame takes up a lot of energy. This energy can be better spent on ourselves and trying to improve our lives. If you are feeling guilty or ashamed of something, first of all have a good think about where the feeling came from. It could be that you are still living by the rules set for you long ago by your family or the society you were living in. The world has become much more tolerant and open-minded. Are you feeling ashamed or guilty about doing something that nowadays wouldn't even raise an eyebrow? Could you not be more tolerant with yourself? Maybe what you did was wicked or bad. But how long do you have to suffer for it? After all, even murderers serve only a few years in prison for what they have done. Isn't it about time you let yourself off the hook? The best you can do is apologise to the people you have hurt and try to clean up the mess you have made. Then you have to learn from the experience and move on.

Sometimes parents, with the best of intentions, can damage us.

Depression and Breakdown

Ruth was brought up by parents who were strict Presbyterians. Their family life was very austere. There were no parties or dancing. In fact, there was very little fun of any kind. Ruth was an obedient and submissive girl; she did not socialise with other children, who were judged by her parents to be bad influences on her. Sex was never discussed in the household. As a result Ruth did not go through the rebellious phase that most girls do in their teenage years. She became a shy and meek woman. She married a dictatorial man who bullied her and made her life a misery. She had grown up with a fear of sex, which, to her, was something sinful, hidden, not to be thought about. As a result she found sex with her husband frightening and dirty. He blamed her for being frigid.

Ruth can now decide for herself what is bad or sinful. She may be able to learn to stand up to her husband, to find pleasure in sex.

Anger and the Desire for Revenge

If you have been treated badly by someone and you are harbouring resentment, how long do you have to do this? If you continue to have these feelings about someone it means that you are carrying them around with you to this day, and dwelling on the hurt they have caused you. This takes a lot of energy. It may be time to let it go and get on with your life, rather than indulging all that old, bad feeling.

What Mid-Life Crisis?

By mid-life we are mature adults. We have another thirty or forty years to live. There is no point in dragging all that old baggage with us into the second half of our lives.

Family Roles

Families often assign different roles to their children. We can be told that we are the 'pretty one' , the 'brainy one', the 'sporty one' or the 'black sheep'. The 'pretty one' will be encouraged to look after her appearance; she will be expected to be flirtatious. That is fine, but she may also not be encouraged to do well at school – after all, 'if you are pretty you can't be brainy too'. The 'brainy one' will believe that she is not attractive and will lose confidence with members of the opposite sex. The 'sporty one' will be admired for his or her performance on the field but may not be encouraged to work at academic subjects. The 'black sheep' will have the hardest time of all. This is the person on whom the rest of the family put all the bad feelings and negativity. They are expected to be bad, that is their function, so that the rest of the family can carry on being 'good'. If you are told that you are 'bad' when you are a child, you believe it and you go out into the world doing 'bad' things.

We believe what we are told when we are children. When you were a child were you told that you were no good at this or that? I was told by my headmistress at the age of 4 that I could not sing and was taken out of the group who were going to sing at an open day at school. For the next fifty-five years I believed that I could not sing. I avoided singing, even when friends were belting out songs at parties. I wouldn't even sing by myself in the bath. Then I went to a voice trainer and found that I can sing. Not very well, but I have missed out on so much practice. I have also missed out on a lot of fun, on opportunities to express myself in song and to develop my appreciation for vocal music.

A friend of mine always got bad marks for art. At the age of 52 she went to university and got a degree in fine arts.

So we have to examine the beliefs we have grown up with and decide now, in the light of the wisdom we have acquired over the years, whether they are true or not. At mid-life we really have to stand back and look at ourselves objectively. Where are we now? What do we want out of life? There is still time to go out and get what we want if we put those old beliefs behind us.

The difficulty is that, if we change, we won't know who we will be. It is a great unknown and it can be frightening. And we have to say goodbye to our past youth. Sometimes it is like going through a period of mourning for what we have lost. We all know people who get stuck in this period of mourning for the past. They live on their memories and are unable to move on. We also have to get over the fear that if we don't fit in we are seen as mad or ill or eccentric. Why should we fit in? It is a world designed for young people, not for us. It is up to us to change it to suit ourselves.

At mid-life death begins to make itself felt. Sometimes people's partners die and leave them with all the tasks of grief and mourning to go through. It is a painful period of loss and sorrow. At this age, too, our parents begin to become frail and to die. We may find ourselves becoming carers. There is a lot of worry and heartache and hard work. This is something we cannot avoid. Eventually, if we can face up to the pain and get through the difficult times, we can come out strengthened and wiser.

The Fear Factor

> Opposition and conflicts are provisionally useful, and teach us to think – people who fear conflict tend, like the lotus-eaters, to be unable to change and to grow up. (Polden, 2002)

Fear, rather than hatred, is the opposite emotion to love. Hate is a strong emotion that keeps us bound to the object of our hatred. It is an active emotion. It can be thrilling, almost as thrilling as love. Fear is different. I am not talking about the rush of emotion we get on a fairground ride, or in a near-miss traffic incident. That is the automatic reaction of our bodies to danger and it can be exciting. What I am talking about here is the cold fear that stops us from moving on. It is a desire for safety. It keeps us in the familiar present rather than the exciting future.

This kind of fear can be so severe that it stops people from leaving their houses. They suffer from agoraphobia and never go out. The same kind of fear stops us from moving away from what is familiar and trying new things. But we have to try new things. It is what we are designed to do. Otherwise, how are we going to develop

What Mid-Life Crisis?

our confidence and abilities? Life is like one of those old-fashioned computer games where you have to jump on to platforms that may go up or go down. You don't know whether the next platform will go up or down but if you don't jump you are not even in the game. Maybe the next thing you do will turn out to be a mistake, but it might also lead to new and exciting things. If you don't jump you will never know.

> *Ken is the Transport Manager in a large haulage firm. He loathes his job. It is very stressful with endless complications and awkward drivers to deal with. If he gets it wrong it costs his firm an awful lot of money. But it is well paid and when he is 65 he will get a very good pension. His job takes up so much of his time and energy that he has little left over for his family life. He is getting very unfit because he is desk-bound all day and he eats a diet of pies and chips from the canteen at work. Last year he had a mild heart attack. It was very frightening. So painful. And he might have died! He was off work for a whole month. But when he came back things had got into such a mess without him that it took ages to sort it all out. He is working just as hard as ever. His wife has suggested that he give it up and take a less stressful job. But then he would lose his pension. It would be an awful lot of money, just thrown away.*

People stay in the same unsatisfactory job because it is safe and familiar. They may stick at it just for the pension.

Family Roles

Security. Having enough money. Is it worth it? Some would say yes. But at what cost? People endure years and years of unhappiness and discontent at home and at work for the sake of security. The constant stress can lead to physical illnesses such as heart disease. What is the point of staying in a safe job or safe relationship if it is going to kill us? We might not even live long enough to draw the pension we have worked so hard for.

Very often, if you really fear something, you can bring it about unconsciously. How often have we seen someone who fears so much that they will lose their partner that they are suspicious when their partner is away from them? They try to control the partner's every move. What happens? Their partner won't put up with the lack of trust and controlling behaviour. It kills their love. We need to learn to focus on the good things in life.

Going Through the Transition

As children we were taught that we had to do what was expected of us. We were not encouraged to look inwards, to our own *internal* authority. We got the idea that as long as we worked hard and stayed on the straight and narrow we would be rewarded. But when we get to mid-life we find that we have been deluded. There seems to be nothing to show for all that obedience and hard work. We realise that we are going to get old and lose everything we have been working for. We won't have a place in society any more. We will be out of the race to make

What Mid-Life Crisis?

money and acquire things. The young people will take over the power we once had. So now we have a difficult task. It is up to us to give ourselves permission to explore new territory. We can now work at things that may not bring us fame and fortune but which we, ourselves, find satisfying and rewarding. We can make new friends and work at better relationships with our old friends and our families. This is a time when we begin to explore our spirituality and our beliefs about what makes life meaningful.

It is very difficult to change. We have been conditioned to fit into society. We have been walking in deeply ingrained ruts. It may not be all that comfortable in those ruts but it is familiar. It is hard and frightening to get off the beaten path and to branch out into new territory. At mid-life the well-trodden paths peter out. There is no established pattern about what we should do and how we should behave. Until recently we have been expected just to get old, stay at home and live a very boring life until we get frail and die. Now most of us are still alert and healthy at mid-life. But few people have gone before us into this new territory. We are the pioneers. It takes a lot of courage to strike out into the unknown.

And we are on our own. When we reach mid-life our parents are becoming elderly and frail or may even have died. They aren't there to protect us any more, or to tell us what to do. It is now our role to look after them. But that also means that we don't have to work to please them any more. We are free to do as we like.

Family Roles

If we are going to be emotionally healthy we have to keep growing and changing. We have to learn from our experiences. And we have to carry on taking an interest in the world around us. If we get stuck we suffer.

Where Do We Go From Here?

- Now that I've done it, what does it all mean?
- What is the purpose of my existence from now on?
- Do I really like the person I turned out to be? Is it too late to change?
- With so many challenges behind me, what makes it worth it to keep trying?
- How will my way of loving change?
- Where do I find a real sense of community?
- How do I build into my life a vehicle for creative expression?
- If I start over again with a second family, will I feel younger or older?
- Or: Without children, how do I remain connected to the future?
- If I haven't made it in earlier career incarnations, is this the end of promise? Or the converse dilemma, what do I do when I've exceeded all my dreams?
- If I don't subscribe to a formal religion, how do I find spiritual comfort?
- Does middle age bring us to the culmination of life? Or is it simply an anticlimax to be endured?
- Will society recognize us as the wise people or cast us aside as superfluous?

(Sheehy, 1995)

Health

> Most men take better care of their cars than their own bodies. At least they take their cars for regular inspections and tune-ups. (Sheehy, 1995)

The first thing we have to do is to look after our health. If we don't we will die sooner rather than later and we will not live to experience the joys of maturity.

It is at mid-life when we find that our bad habits have caught up with us. We have put on weight, our arteries are furred up, we are developing diabetes, our lungs are clogged up with tar from smoking, we are getting decrepit. The worst thing we can do when this starts to happen is to sit back and claim, 'I can't do that any more, I am too old'. An attitude like that is the beginning of the end. Once we start to slow down we will grind to a halt much more quickly. We will never have the opportunity to enjoy our old age – or even our late middle age. At mid-life it is not too late to put most things right. It is never too late to change our diet, to eat plenty of fruit and vegetables and fewer fatty foods. A change of diet will make us much more healthy and active. It will give us more energy so that we can enjoy our lives. It will build up our immune system so that we will not be so prone to catching illnesses. We will be slimmer and fitter. Even if we do suffer from chronic illnesses, aches and pains or even arthritis, losing weight and maintaining a healthy diet will make it much easier for us to move about and keep active.

Where Do We Go From Here?

It is important to take exercise. The slower we go the slower we will want to go until we come to a full stop. It is vital to get out and do something: go for regular walks, go down the gym, take up dancing or a sport. Anything to keep us off that settee of an evening. It will help prolong our lives and make living so much more enjoyable. Exercise fills our brains with endorphins which make us feel happy. It has the same effect as eating chocolate has for some people, or taking drugs. So, if we exercise regularly we will be happier.

It is even more important for men to have a good diet because it is accepted that they have a shorter life span than women. There are still plenty of men who live to a ripe old age, so men need to make an extra effort to stay fit and healthy. But tradition has it that men should be well fed with rich food. In the past it was important for the breadwinner to be strong and he was given the best food, even in times of famine. That does not apply in this Western world of plenty. It just means that men become fat and unfit. In today's society machines can do so much that there are fewer manual jobs for men to do. Most men's work is done sitting or standing. How often does a woman go on a diet but carry on serving the old fatty stuff to her family! It is considered un-masculine to eat healthy food. Men laugh at their colleagues who eat healthily, claiming that they are being bullied by their wives. Many men seem to be proud of their fat bellies. Perhaps it is a sign of stability and the ability to provide food for the family, or maybe proof that they can afford large quantities of beer or rich food. Maybe being thin and healthy is connected with manual labour. A fat man can't possibly be doing a manual job. Whatever the reasons, they are out of date and it is time men changed their ideas before it is too late.

Men have nothing to lose and everything to gain by changing their diets. Not only will they live longer, suffer fewer illnesses and feel fitter, but they will have better sex lives. One of the main causes of impotence in men is poor circulation caused by cholesterol in the arteries. Diabetes also causes problems with impotence, as does being fat and lazy.

Men will live longer and healthier lives if they keep themselves fit. So many men spend their spare time in front of the television or down at the pub. Yet there are many more enjoyable things to do: walking, cycling, various sports, dancing. Many British men seem to be afraid of making fools of themselves on the dance floor but they don't have to go to night clubs. There are hundreds of dance classes taking place every night where they can learn anything from jive to ballroom dancing. There are always spare women and new male members are welcomed.

Women at mid-life are generally fitter than men. They are usually the ones who do all the housework, so they are constantly running around with vacuum cleaners, dusters and mops. They are changing beds, cooking, ironing, shopping (how many men sit in the car while their partner does the grocery shopping?). This helps them to keep fit, even before they take any extra exercise. One of the good results of today's consumer society is that

Where Do We Go From Here?

women are encouraged to be slim and fit. It is probably one of the reasons why women live longer than men.

We have to keep our brains healthy too. The brain is like the body: it needs regular exercise to keep it in good trim. We have to stay interested in what is going on around us, we have to keep reading, exercising our brain by doing crosswords, number puzzles, writing – better still, studying. Otherwise we start to become like those despised 'little old men' or 'little old women' who we talk down to as if they are stupid. If we don't use our brains we become slow.

If, by this time of life, we are suffering from chronic illness, we must do the best we can to manage it and not to despair. Our state of mind can make a big difference to how we feel. If we keep a positive attitude and distract ourselves with things that interest us, we can make the illness more bearable.

The Joys of Mid-Life!

The rules and expectations of society have been made for young people. As mentioned before in this book, the present mid-life generation is the first one ever to have reached this stage in life while staying active and healthy. There is no need for us to live by younger people's rules. We can do as we like.

Women who have gone through the menopause will be experiencing the vitality, the surge of well being that comes after their periods have stopped. And they are free from the constant worry about whether a period is starting or whether they might get pregnant, after forty or so years of being careful – or not being careful and getting caught out!

There are no patterns as to how to behave as a woman of today. We are breaking new ground. Girls are taking the initiative in relationships, asking for dates, demanding sex. We even have girl gangs terrorising our inner cities. Women are rising to dizzy heights in the corporate world. There is very little to stop us now.

Men often have a more difficult time at mid-life. They are used to having status and being in charge. Now their wives or partners have suddenly become energetic and assertive. Older men are being passed over for promotion in their work in favour of younger people. A lot of men are being requested to retire early. Many men have already discovered this, as Jim and Sally Conway say in their book *Women in Midlife Crisis*: 'Companies are keen to recruit young people and many start to weed out mid-life people – why? Because the older, more mature people will not play their games – get tired of their ethos of keen, ruthless competition, both in the market place and inside their own companies' (Jim and Sally Conway, 1983).

With loss of job comes loss of status. This takes some getting used to. At this stage in life it is very important for men to give up their old values. No longer can they keep their position by being physically strong and forceful. Even their sexual prowess is beginning to fail. They must start to look for other satisfactions in life. They need to develop their ability to love, not just sex but caring and intimacy. They need to take an interest in other people and use their experience to mentor and help them.

Men really must give up the macho culture and become more mature. Once they have done this they, like women, experience an enormous sense of freedom. The old culture gives them a great deal of responsibility, not only for their wives and families but for the people who work for them. Now they are on a more equal footing with their partners, their children are grown and they are free to pursue anything that interests them. It is even more important for men, as they do not live as long as women so they don't have as much time to fit in everything that they want to do. They really have to get on with it. In doing so, they may find that they escape the physical and psychological factors that lead to men's early death.

For both sexes this is an opportunity to go back to parts of our lives that we may not have completed. For example, we may not have been able to indulge in riotous living in our adolescence, buying sports cars, finding young sexual partners, behaving irresponsibly. Well, we can do that now if we want to. And maybe that needs to be played out before we are ready to start maturing again. There are lots of middle-aged people on the lists of dating agencies, going on singles holidays, visiting singles clubs. And many of them can afford to travel and entertain when, in their younger days, they could not. But if both partners are open to change there may be no need to split up. If one partner can allow the other to go off and catch up with lost parts of themselves, there is a good chance that they will come back eventually. They can learn to love one another all over again, they can learn to respect the other and take an interest in what they are doing while, at the same time, allowing them freedom to continue to learn and mature.

Many people at this time go back to college or to university to study those things that have always interested them. They make much better students than their adolescent fellow students. They bring a wealth of experience with them. Life has given them shocks and tragedy and made them wiser. After years of experience mid-life people are more resilient and able to take the shocks of life. They can take in their stride things that would have worried them in their younger years. Bringing up children has forced them to consider others before themselves. If they are lucky they have learned to manage feelings, their own and those of their children. People find that they have a better perspective on life: 'Having almost certainly failed at some major personal or professional challenge and found they didn't die from it, they are in general more efficient and effective in the way they go about their lives' (Sheehy, 1995).

Friends are very important at this time of life. Most women are used to having good friends with whom they can discuss their intimate concerns and feelings, but men often find themselves having different, more caring relationships with their good friends, sharing in life's sorrows and tragedies as well as its pleasures. They are called upon to mentor younger men and give the benefit of their experience. Talking about our problems helps us

Where Do We Go From Here?

to deal with them and helps us to become emotionally healthy. We learn that by giving support, we also receive it. We also learn to treat people in the way we would like to be treated. We learn to make ourselves available to friends in difficulty, to show empathy and understanding – to become less self-centred and judgemental. We are less likely to make assumptions about people, more likely to be more tolerant and to look for the good in them, rather than assuming the worst. We are able to learn from difficult situations and to decide, if things go wrong, how we would tackle a similar situation in the future.

We learn to avoid the 'all-or-nothing' approach to life:

- If something didn't work once – it never will again
- If somebody is unkind to you once – they are an unkind person
- If somebody doesn't want to do something to help you once – they never will again
- If a partner lets you down – nobody is trustworthy

By now we have learned to tolerate other people's failings – and our own.

At mid-life we can't judge people by how they look. Everybody by this stage is looking a bit ragged around the edges. Now we can't hide behind the beauty we once had. We have to let people see who the real person is underneath.

By now we have learned that if we want others to treat us in a certain way, it is not a bad idea to begin by treating them in just that self-same way ourselves. 'We become increasingly able to take pleasure in others' achievements, to desire their well-being as well as our own' (Polden, 2002). We are able to show empathy and understanding, even if we disapprove of how people have been behaving (Milne, 2004). Having suffered pain ourselves we become more sensitive to the pain of others.

> Midlife is the point where we recognize the end of unlimited promise and the fact that we *cannot control* many of the *bad things* that happen to us. . . . But we should also recognise that we do have increasing control over the good things that happen to us. (Sheehy, 1995, emphasis in original)

The most important thing we have to do is to live life more consciously. We are aware that it is passing quickly and we have to make the most of what we have left. We have to learn to look inside ourselves for solutions to our problems. This is the time to let go of painful periods in our past, of bitterness and negativity. We need to examine the feelings of failure and disappointment and let them go.

> Once this worst has been faced up to, we may find – often to our surprise – that those needs for approval and protection which shaped so many of the choices of our childhood, adolescence and early adulthood and seemed an inalienable part of living, begin to fade away. (Polden, 2002)

Where Do We Go From Here?

We need to be able to spend quiet time on our own to allow realisations to come up from within. In this way we come to terms with loss and let go of things we have been clinging on to. We learn to confront reality and the changes that are taking place within us and around us. When we are able to do this we become mature; as Gail Sheehy says, 'The transformation of middle life is to move into a more stable psychological state of mastery, where we control much of what happens in our life and can often act on the world, rather than habitually react to whatever the world throws at us' (Sheehy, 1995).

At mid-life we must find the time to indulge our interests. When we are young our energy goes into making things to sell to one another and there seems to be no kind of higher purpose. There is nothing telling us that it might be a good idea to go fishing or take up sculpting. Nobody will make any money out of that. Dr Brice Pitt, in *Making the Most of Middle Age*, says, 'Hobbies need to be seen less as filling time than as feeding the soul' (Pitt, 1980). A hobby is an activity that absorbs us, that takes us away from the mundane world, that enables us to get some peace or to use our creativity. It is a spiritual thing. David Fontana, in his book *Discover Zen*, says:

> The Zen state is created by a frame of mind rather than by anything intrinsic to the activity itself. As beginners, then, we are more likely to attain it when we are absorbed in a pleasurable activity, such as a hobby. At such times we become oblivious to everything going on

What Mid-Life Crisis?

around us – unaware of the passage of time, of physical sensations such as hunger or discomfort, of noises and disturbances. All existence is contained in the activity. (Fontana, 2001)

At mid-life, with the realisation that death is inevitable, people start to ask big questions: What is life all about? What am I here for, really? It can't be merely to shop, to keep the economy going. It is at this time that they begin to look for spiritual guidance to help them through the remainder of their lives. Many people find the dogma of established religions distasteful and bigotry repulsive. This can leave people in a quandary. They find themselves on their own with no guidance, other than an innate feeling that there is a spiritual aspect to life. This is why there is such a resurgence of interest in the spiritual foundations of the old religions, such as Gnosticism and Sufism, and in everyday phenomena that can be found in practices such as spiritualism, astrology, faith healing, tarot, reading auras, and so on. To stay on the spiritual path, people should keep an open mind and carry on with the search. Otherwise, in the words of Jane Polden, 'Then ... we turn away from our own deepest needs with anger or cynicism and give up the search, reverting back to the worn habits of first adulthood or shrinking in on ourselves in depression' (Polden, 2002).

This is a time to get out in all weathers. Notice the seasons. Many of us live in our own little worlds, totally divorced from the Earth. Now is the time to connect with the rhythms of the seasons, of life, to turn the lights out and experience darkness for a while, to notice which phase the moon is in, to recognise that we are alive and part of a larger whole.

The best way I can sum up the qualities we need for a satisfactory life is to quote Carl Rogers' list:

- openness
- desire for authenticity
- scepticism regarding science and technology
- a desire for wholeness
- the wish for intimacy
- being a 'process person'
- caring
- having a positive attitude towards nature
- is anti-institutional
- acknowledges the authority within
- the unimportance of material things
- has a yearning for the spiritual

(Rogers, 1980)

If we can aspire to gain these qualities and work hard at keeping them we can enter this new phase of our life with joy and a sense of adventure.

Bibliography

BUPA Factsheet, www.bupa.co.uk (April 2007)
Conway, J., 1978: *Men in Mid Life Crisis* (David C. Cook Publishing Co.)
Conway, J. and Conway, S., 1983: *Women in Midlife Crisis* (Tyndale House Publishers, Inc., Illinois)
Erikson, E. H., 1985: *The Life Cycle Completed* (W. W. Norton & Company Ltd)
Fontana, D., 2001: *Discover Zen* (Chronicle Books LLC, San Francisco)
Freud, S., 1912: *On the Universal Tendency to Debasement in the Sphere of Love* (Penguin Freud Library 7)
Gibran, K., 1991: *The Prophet* (Pan Books)
Hildebrand, P., 1995: *Beyond Mid-Life Crisis* (Sheldon Press)
Hillman, J., 1983: *Inter Views* (Spring Publications Inc.)
Hollis, J., 1993: *The Middle Passage: From Misery to Meaning in Midlife* (Inner City Books, Toronto)
Jung, C. G., 1973: *Letters* (Bollingen Series XCV), 2 vols. Trans. R. F. C. Hull, ed. G. Adler and A. Jaffe (Princeton University Press)
Jung, C. G., 2001: *Modern Man in Search of a Soul* (Routledge Classics)
Mascaro, J. (trans.), 1973: *The Dhammapada* (Penguin Classics)
Milne, D., 2004: *Coping with a Mid-Life Crisis* (Sheldon Press)

Nemiroff, R. A., M. D. and Colarusso, C. A., M. D., 1985: *The Race Against Time: Psychotherapy and Psychoanalysis in the Second Half of Life* (Plenum Press)

Pirsig, R. M., 1974: *Zen and the Art of Motorcycle Maintenance* (Vintage)

Pitt, B., M. D., 1980: *Making the Most of Middle Age* (Sheldon Press)

Polden, J., 2002: *Regeneration: Journey Through the Mid-Life Crisis* (Continuum International)

Rogers, C., 1980: *A Way of Being* (Houghton Mifflin)

Sheehy, G., 1976: *Passages: Predictable Crises of Adult Life* (Bantam Books)

Sheehy, G., 1991: *Menopause:The Silent Passage* (Pocket Books, Simon & Schuster Inc.)

Sheehy, G., 1995: *New Passages: Mapping Your Life Across Time* (Ballantine Books)

About the Author

Celia Dawson was born in 1948. After a childhood spent in Lancashire she attended universtity in Bangor, North Wales, gaining a Degree in English and French. On leaving university she married and eventually settled in West Yorkshire where she worked as a secretary. She had a great interest in young people and worked in youth clubs in the evenings. When her first child was born she gave up her office job but continued with her youth work.

In 1993 Celia took a counselling course to help her with her youth work and found it so fascinating that she went on to become a qualified counsellor and manager of a counselling charity. She is now divorced and actively pursuing personal development and spiritual interests.

For further information about Celia log on to her website at: www.celiadawsonlifecoach.com